www.raintreepublishers.co.uk
Visit our website to find out more information about Raintree books.

To order:
☎ Phone 0845 6044371
🖷 Fax +44 (0) 1865 312263
🖳 Email myorders@raintreepublishers.co.uk

Customers from outside the UK please telephone +44 1865 312262

Raintree is an imprint of Capstone Global Library Limited, a company incorporated in England and Wales having its registered office at 7 Pilgrim Street, London, EC4V 6LB – Registered company number: 6695582

Edited by Megan Cotugno, Louise Galpine, and Abby Colich
Designed by Richard Parker
Original illustrations © Capstone Global Library Ltd (2010)
Illustrated by Darren Lingard
Picture research by Mica Brancic
Originated by Capstone Global Library Ltd
Printed in China by CTPS

ISBN 978 0 431085 21 0 (hardback)
14 13 12 11 10
10 9 8 7 6 5 4 3 2 1

British Library Cataloguing in Publication Data
Rand, Casey
Time. – (Measure it!)
A full catalogue record for this book is available from the British Library.

Acknowledgements
We would like to thank the following for permission to reproduce photographs: Alamy p. **14** (©Artostock.com); Corbis pp. **12** (©Martyn Goddard), **23** (Loop Images/ LOOP IMAGES/© Neil Tingle), **25** (Science Faction/© Scott Andrews), **26** (©Louie Psihoyos); Getty Images pp. **4** (Stockbyte), **21** (Jeff Gross), **27** (Visuals Unlimited/Jeff Daly); iStockphoto pp. **7** (©Robert Simon), **8** (NASA); Rex Features p. **16** (Alisdair Macdonald); Shutterstock p. **5** (©Henry Tsui), **9** (©Martine Oger).

Cover photo of stopwatch against cog and gear wills reproduced with permission from Photolibrary (David Muri).

We would like to thank John Pucek for his invaluable help in the preparation of this book.

Every effort has been made to contact copyright holders of material reproduced in this book. Any omissions will be rectified in subsequent printings if notice is given to the publishers.

Disclaimer
All the Internet addresses (URLs) given in this book were valid at the time of going to press. However, due to the dynamic nature of the Internet, some addresses may have changed, or sites may have changed or ceased to exist since publication. While the author and publisher regret any inconvenience this may cause readers, no responsibility for any such changes can be accepted by either the author or the publisher.

Contents

Some words are printed in bold, **like this**. You can find out what they mean by looking in the glossary on page 30.

What is time?

The day is here. The hour is at hand. The minute is upon us. The time has come. Three, two, one, it's time to learn about time!

Time is all around us. Everything we do takes time. Time is a measure of the **interval** between two events. There is an interval between when school starts on Monday, and when it starts on Tuesday. Time helps us to describe the length of this interval. Time describes this interval as 24 hours, or one day.

Why do we measure time?

What would happen if you didn't have a clock and you just went to school whenever you thought the time was right? Do you think you would arrive at the right time every day? If your classmates also did not have clocks, do you think you would all arrive for school at the same time? Measuring time helps us to know when we need to be somewhere. We need a way to keep track of when certain events are taking place so we can be at the right place at the right time. This is why we measure time.

Measuring time allows you and your classmates to know when to arrive at school in the morning.

Remember the saying that "time flies when you are having fun"? As you read, try to answer the questions, complete the activities, and have fun. You will be done in no time, and you will know all about measuring time!

Did you know?
A **jiffy** is a brief **period** of time lasting approximately 1/100 of a second.

How is time divided?

A day is divided into hours, minutes, and seconds no matter where you are. However, it's never the same time in London as it is in New York City, USA. To make one system for measuring time work everywhere, the world was divided into 24 **time zones**.

24 hours in a day

Each morning the sun appears to rise in the eastern sky. As Earth rotates, the sun appears to move across the sky. Each night the sun appears to set, or disappear in the western sky. A day is based on Earth's rotation and the appearance of the sun moving across the sky. But why are days divided into 24 hours?

A day divided

Over 3,500 years ago, ancient Egyptians divided the day into 12 equal parts and the night into 12 equal parts. We have used 24 parts, or hours, to divide each day ever since.

> **Did you know?**
> Many ancient Greeks believed that the sun was actually a god named Helios. They believed Helios rode a fiery chariot across the sky each day.

a.m. and p.m.

In some parts of the world, **12-hour time** is used. This means that each day is divided into two 12-hour parts. The first 12 hours of the day are followed by the letters **a.m.**, for example 6:00 a.m. The second 12-hour **period** of each day is followed by the letters **p.m.**, for example 11:00 p.m.

- a.m. stands for the Latin word *ante meridiem*, meaning before midday
- p.m. stands for *post meridiem*, meaning past midday.

24-hour time

Some parts of the world use **24-hour time**. Instead of using a.m. and p.m., they divide the day into 24 parts. See how they compare in the table below.

12- and 24-hour time

12-hour	midnight	1:00 a.m.	2:00 a.m.	3:00 a.m.	4:00 a.m.	5:00 a.m.	6:00 a.m.	7:00 a.m.	8:00 a.m.	9:00 a.m.	10:00 a.m.	11:00 a.m.
24-hour	0000 or 2400	0100	0200	0300	0400	0500	0600	0700	0800	0900	1000	1100
12-hour	noon	1:00 p.m.	2:00 p.m.	3:00 p.m.	4:00 p.m.	5:00 p.m.	6:00 p.m.	7:00 p.m.	8:00 p.m.	9:00 p.m.	10:00 p.m.	11:00 p.m.
24-hour	1200	1300	1400	1500	1600	1700	1800	1900	2000	2100	2200	2300

As Earth rotates, our view of the sun changes from the rising morning sun in the east, the high overhead sun of midday, and the falling evening sun in the west.

The world united

Many years ago, people in most towns and cities decided what time they should set their own clocks. This was based on where the sun appeared to be in the sky each day. Once travel and communication from place to place became faster with the invention of trains and telegrams, this method became confusing. To travel on trains moving from place to place and to communicate with people in places far away, people needed a common way to keep track of time everywhere.

Universal time

When people around the world decided that they needed a shared way to keep track of time, they agreed to make the time in Greenwich, London, the standard for their shared time. The time in Greenwich became the **universal time**. It is the time on which clocks around the world were based. It is known as **Greenwich Mean Time (GMT)**.

While the sun is already shining on the eastern United States each morning, it is still dark on the western United States.

The world divided

As Earth rotates, the sun shines on different parts of Earth at different times. As the morning sun is rising in Australia, it is getting dark in Edinburgh. So if it was the same time everywhere in the world, midnight would be very sunny in some places! To solve this problem, time zones were introduced. Time zones are the 24 divisions of Earth based on a series of imaginary lines that run from the north pole to the south pole. These lines are known as **lines of longitude**.

Time zone maps

This time zone map shows the 24 divisions of Earth used for measuring time. Each column or vertical bar on the map represents a different time zone. The top and bottom of each bar tells you how many hours to add or subtract from the GMT to work out the time in that bar. Remember that clocks around the world are based on GMT. Can you tell what time it is in Chicago when the GMT is midnight?

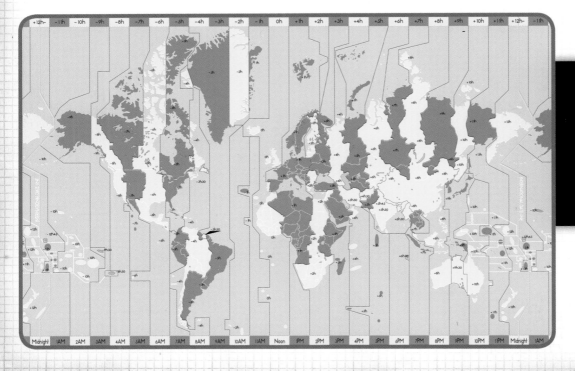

This map shows how the world is divided into 24 time zones.

Why does a week have seven days?

A day is based on one rotation of Earth. But from where did the seven-day week come? Historians have many theories about how the seven-day week got started. In early religious texts, God creates the world in six days and rests on the seventh day. The seven-day week has been used since the Roman emperor Constantine made Christianity the official religion of Rome thousands of years ago.

What are the days of the week named after?

One possibility is that the names of the seven days of the week come from the sun, the moon, and the five closest planets: Mercury, Venus, Mars, Jupiter, and Saturn.

Many historians believe that the days of the week are named after the sun, the moon, and the five closest planets.

Sunday: Sun

Monday: Moon

Tuesday: Mars

Wednesday: Mercury

Thursday: Jupiter

Friday: Venus

Saturday: Saturn

Why are there 365 days in a year?

Like a day, a year is also a measurement of time based on an **interval**. A year is the **period** of time it takes for Earth to make a full revolution around the sun. During the time it takes Earth to make one full revolution around the sun, Earth rotates on its axis slightly more than 365 times.

Leap years

Leap years are those years with 366 days, instead of the usual 365. Leap years are necessary because the actual length of time it takes Earth to revolve around the sun is about 365 and ¼ days. Leap years occur every 4 years and have 366 days. This extra day is added to the calendar on 29 February.

Did you know?
A **galactic year** is a period of time lasting 230 million Earth years. This is the time it takes the sun to orbit the Milky Way galaxy.

A year is the period of time it takes for Earth to make one full revolution around the sun.

What do we use to measure time?

Throughout history, humans have developed many different instruments to help keep track of time. Some of them you can even build yourself.

Sundials

A **sundial** is a time-keeping instrument that has been used for thousands of years. It measures time based on the position of the sun in the sky. Most sundials use a long straight stick or rod that stands upright. The sun casts a shadow from the stick onto a flat surface that is marked with lines or numbers that indicate the hours of the day. Throughout the day, the sun moves across the sky and the edge of the shadow moves across the sundial. As the shadow moves across the sundial, the shadow points to different hour markings.

The sun creates a shadow to display the time on this sundial.

Build your own sundial

Materials you will need:
- stick or rod
- 12 small rocks, all about the same size
- a watch or a clock.

Instructions:
1. Find a sunny and flat area to build your sundial.
2. Put the tip of the stick in the ground so the stick stands straight up.
3. Gather 10–12 stones for your sundial.
4. Use a clock to find the time throughout the day. At each hour, place a rock on the ground to mark where the shadow from the stick falls.

Once all of the hours are marked with rocks, your sundial is ready to use. Whenever you want to know the time just look at the shadow and see where it is pointing. Can you read the time on the sundial below?

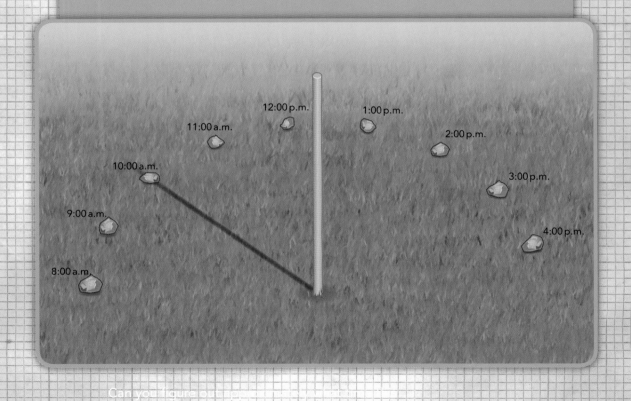

Can you figure out approximately what time the sundial is reading?

Pendulum clocks

A **pendulum clock** uses a swinging object to keep time. The first pendulum clock was accurate to within one minute a day!

How do pendulum clocks work? A pendulum is an object that swings back and forth. The length of time it takes the pendulum to swing back and forth is called the **period**. The period of the pendulum is always **constant** as long as the pendulum keeps swinging. A weight and gears inside the clock keep the pendulum swinging.

The period of a pendulum clock is usually one second. The period of the pendulum's swing keeps the time. The weight pulls to keep the pendulum swinging. When the weight in the clock gets pulled close to the bottom of the clock, the clock owner must wind the clock, pulling the weight back up to its starting position.

pendulum

Testing time

A pendulum swings at a constant rate that depends only on the length of the pendulum and the force of gravity. You can prove this by building your own simple pendulum. Follow the directions on the next page.

A good pendulum clock can keep time very well on a steady surface.

Build your own pendulum clock

You will need:
- a small weight
- a few books
- some string
- a table
- a ruler

Directions:
1. Tie the string to the weight.
2. Put the other end of the string on the table weighted down by heavy books.
3. Pull the weight of the pendulum to the side about 30 centimetres (12 inches).
4. Release the weight.
5. Count how many times the pendulum swings back and forth in 30 seconds.

Repeat steps 3 to 5, but this time only pull the weight of the pendulum back about 15 centimetres (6 inches) and then release. Can you guess what will happen? Remember, a pendulum is good at keeping time because the period of the pendulum is constant. You will find that whether you pull the weight back a lot or a little, the pendulum you built will swing back and forth at a constant rate!

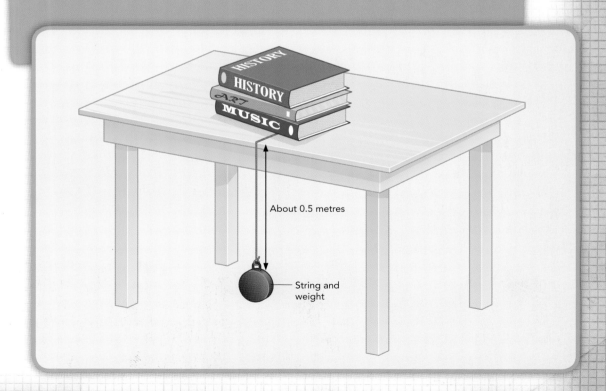

About 0.5 metres

String and weight

Shipwrecked

Early navigation at sea required sailors to find their position using time. Unfortunately, the pendulum clock was not accurate at sea because of the tossing and tilting of the ship. For each minute that a sailor's clock was off, the sailor would be 24 kilometres (15 miles) off course! This error led to hundreds of ship wrecks and lost sailors.

A seaworthy clock

In 1714 the British Parliament offered a cash reward to the inventor of a clock that was accurate at sea. Nearly 50 years later, clock maker John Harrison (1693–1776) finally succeeded in creating an accurate sea clock called the H4. The H4 was a small clock that used springs and balances to overcome the problems with previous clocks at sea. In six weeks at sea, the H4 was accurate within about 6 seconds!

The H4 clock (far left) ticks five times per second and can keep time even on unsteady surfaces.

Digital and analogue clocks

Today, we mainly use **digital clocks** and **analogue clocks**. The first clock below is an example of an analogue clock. Most analogue clock faces have a thick and short hour hand and a thin and long minute hand. To tell the time, you need to read the hour hand first. Decide the number or division that the hour hand last passed. On the clock below, the hour hand has just passed the six. Now we need to look at the minute hand. Each number on the clock face represents 5 minutes. On the clock to the right, the minute hand is pointing to the two. This means two 5-minute periods have passed this hour. It is 6:10.

Digital clocks are easier to read. They show the time in numbers.

Work it out

The digital clock to the right reads 7:15. Draw an analogue clock on a separate piece of paper that reads 7:15.

How much time has passed?

As the hands on the clock go around, time is elapsing. Elapsing is a fancy way of saying passing. **Elapsed time** means the same as time passed. It is very important for you to be able to work out elapsed time.

Tick tock

Can you look at the hands of a clock and tell how much time has elapsed since the last time you looked? On both of the clocks below, the hour hand is between the five and the six. However, the minute hand has moved from the three to the eight. Remember that each number the minute hand passes is five minutes. So how much time has elapsed between the first clock and the second? The minute hand has moved five numbers, each worth five minutes. Twenty-five minutes have elapsed!

Did you know?
In one year, there are 12 months of elapsed time, which means about 52 weeks, or 365 days, or 8,760 hours, or 525,600 minutes, or 31,536,000 seconds! You can see how much time elapses in some other time **periods** in the table below.

Time period	Elapsed time	Time period	Elapsed time
jiffy	$\frac{1}{100}$ seconds	month	28–31 days
second	100 jiffies	quarter-year	4 months
minute	60 seconds	year	12 months
quarter-hour	15 minutes	quinquennium	5 years
hour	60 minutes	decade	10 years
day	24 hours	century	100 years
week	7 days	millennium	1,000 years

Work it out

Can you tell how much time has elapsed between these two clocks? Make sure you pay special attention to the hour hand. Every number the hour hand passes is worth an hour of elapsed time. You have to add this to the amount of elapsed minutes you get from the minute hand. Check your answer on page 29.

How do you master time?

To become a master of measuring time, you need to know how to precisely measure time, how to find the speed of something using **elapsed time**, and how to find the **average** time. Keep reading and you can be a master in no time.

Get ready, get set, go!

Sometimes you will need to measure time very precisely. In the table below are the men's 100-metre gold medal winners from the last five Olympic Games. Each runner finished the 100 metres in between 9 and 10 seconds. If we measured time with an ordinary clock, we could never know who ran the race the fastest.

Men's Olympic 100-metre race winners

Year	Name	Country	Time (seconds)
1992	Linford Christie	Great Britain	9.96
1996	Donovan Bailey	Canada	9.84
2000	Maurice Greene	United States	9.87
2004	Justin Gatlin	United States	9.85
2008	Usain Bolt	Jamaica	9.69

Stopwatches

Sometimes, a tool more precise than an ordinary clock is needed to measure time. In the 100 metre race, a stopwatch is used. It can measure time as precisely as 1/100 of a second. This allows us to know who really ran the fastest and this person's precise time.

How fast was it?

We can use elapsed time to work out speed. To determine speed, use this formula: speed = distance ÷ elapsed time. To determine how fast Usain Bolt ran during the 2008 Olympics, put the information from the previous page into the formula.

speed = distance ÷ elapsed time

speed = 100 metres ÷ 9.69 seconds

speed = 9.69 metres per second

On your marks, get set, go! Don't blink because these men are fast. We need a very precise instrument to measure time in this race.

Making multiple measurements

Sometimes measuring something once is not enough. If we need a very accurate measure of something, we will need to make multiple measurements and then find the average time.

Work it out

If you wanted to know how long tennis matches usually last, you would need to measure the length of several matches to find the average. Look at the table below. If you measured only match 4, your estimate would be too high. If you measured match 1, your estimate would be too low. However, if you measured the length of five matches and found the average, you would have a much more accurate estimate. To find the average time, add the time of each match together and divide by the total number of matches. Can you find the average time? Check your answer on page 29.

Match	Time
1	70 minutes
2	120 minutes
3	100 minutes
4	150 minutes
5	110 minutes

Determining the average time of a tennis match requires multiple measurements to be accurate.

Constants and variables

In some calculations, time is a **constant**, and in others it is a **variable**. A constant is a quantity whose value does not change in a measurement. A variable is a quantity that can change in each measurement.

If you measure how far each of your friends can run in 40 seconds, the distance of each run would vary. Some may run 200 metres in 40 seconds, while others would run only 100 metres. But both would be running for 40 seconds. Here time, 40 seconds, is a constant, while the distance is a variable.

If you measured how quickly each of your friends could run 200 metres, the time would vary for each. Time would be a variable. Some would finish in 40 seconds while other would take 50 seconds. The distance, 200 metres, would be a constant.

Is time travel possible?

We are all moving forwards in time. Every day, we all get one day older. But what about moving forwards faster in time or moving backwards in time? Is it possible?

Travelling to the future

Scientist Albert Einstein (1879–1955) developed the **theory of special relativity** that tells us about the possibility of time travel. This theory states that when travelling at speeds near the speed of light, time slows down. The speed of light is 300,000 kilometres per second (186,000 miles per second). So, if a ship that travels near this speed is ever built, time would slow down for the passengers of the ship.

Slowing down time

According to Einstein's theory, if you left Earth in a spaceship at the age of 12 and travelled at the speed of light for 2 years, you would return to Earth at 14 years old. However, the people on Earth would have aged much more than 2 years. When you return, your friends might be 30 years old! Time slowed down for you but not for them. You aged 2 years, while they might have aged 18 years. You would have travelled into time. Now, how do you get back?

Space travel today

During some space missions today, astronauts have to account for the theory of special relativity. These space ships don't travel nearly the speed of light, but they do travel very fast, and time does slow down for the astronauts a very tiny amount. The clocks that go into space on these missions always return to Earth a few seconds behind clocks on Earth. In a way, we have already started to time travel, just not very much!

Space shuttles travel at very high speeds. On these spaceships, time slows down a very small amount, confirming Einstein's theory of special relativity.

How do scientists measure when dinosaurs lived?

The word **dinosaur** comes from the Greek for "terrible, fearful lizard". Dinosaurs were huge lizards that ruled Earth for millions of years. But how do scientists **estimate** when dinosaurs lived?

Estimating the age of fossils

Fossils are the remains of plants and animals that have died a long time ago. Scientists try to work out how old fossils are using **relative dating** and **absolute dating**.

Most dinosaurs lived on Earth over 65 million years ago.

Relative dating is a way for scientists to estimate how old fossils are by looking at the rock and soil surrounding a fossil. Layers of rock build up on Earth's crust over long **periods** of time. Since newer layers of rock usually form on top of older layers, scientists can estimate which fossils are the oldest and newest based on what layer of rock the fossils are found in.

Radioactive elements are those that are naturally going through a type of change that gives off energy. These radioactive elements change at a very predictable rate. These elements allow scientists to measure the age of an object by looking at how much of the radioactive elements in the fossil have already changed. Since scientists know approximately how fast these elements change, knowing how many have already changed gives them a good approximation of the fossils age. This is known as absolute dating.

Other types of fossils

Not all fossils are found in rocks. Some animals in the past were trapped in natural tar pits where they are preserved. Animals that lived during the ice ages were sometimes frozen in ice or frozen soil. Some extinct insects have been found trapped in sap from fossilized trees.

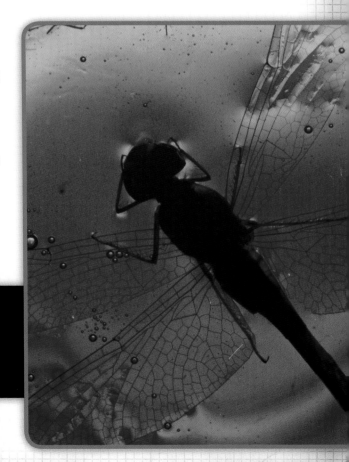

The sap from fossilized trees is called amber. Insects fossilized in amber are very well preserved.

A timeline of time

Tools to measure time more accurately are always being developed. Below is a timeline that lists some of the major events in time measurement. We create timelines to make information more interesting and easier to read. Timelines show a sequence of related events arranged in **chronological order** and displayed along a line. Chronological order means that the events are arranged in order from first to last based on when in time they happened.

Time	Event
1500 BCE	First **sundial** is used in Egypt.
325 BCE	Greeks use a water clock to measure time.
46 BCE	Julius Caesar develops a solar calendar and **leap years**.
875 CE	Alfred the Great uses burning candles to measure time.
1335	First mechanical clock is built.
1583	Galileo develops the idea for a **pendulum clock**.
1656	Christiaan Huygens builds the first accurate pendulum clock.
1759	John Harrison builds the first clock that is accurate at sea.
1905	A radio time signal is transmitted from Washington, D.C., USA, to help ships find their position.
1927	Joseph Horton and Warren Marrison build the first quartz crystal oscillator clock.
1967	A second is defined as 9,192,631,770 vibrations of the cesium atom.
1983	Radio-controlled clocks become common in Europe.
1994	Radio-controlled clocks become common in the United States.
2001	Optical atomic clock that "ticks" one quadrillion times per second is created!

Answers to "Work it out"

What instruments are used to measure time? (page 17)

Your drawing should look like this:

How much time has passed? (page 19)

One hour and 15 minutes of time has elapsed between the two clocks.

How do you master time? (page 22)

Add 70, 120, 100, 150, and 110 together to get 550. Divide this by 5. The average tennis match is 110 minutes.

Glossary

12-hour time time that divides the day into two 12-hour parts

24-hour time time that divides the day into 24 parts

absolute dating way of finding the age of fossils using radioactive decay

a.m. abbreviation for the Latin word *ante meridiem*, meaning before midday

analogue clock type of clock that measures time using hands that point to the present time

chronological order arrangement starting from first occurrence to last occurrence

constant value that does not change

digital clock clock that displays a numeric representation of time

elapsed time amount of time that has passed or gone by

estimate to make an approximate judgement about something

fossil remains of a plant or animal preserved in earth or rock

galactic year duration of time required for the sun to orbit the Milky Way galaxy

Greenwich Mean Time the time in Greenwich, London, which is used as the basis time throughout the world

interval period of time between two events

jiffy one one-hundredth of a second

leap year year in which an extra day is added to keep the calendar and seasons in rhythm

line of longitude imaginary line that runs from the north pole to the south pole

pendulum clock clock that uses a pendulum to keep time

period length of time required for the back and forth motion of a pendulum clock to complete a cycle

p.m. abbreviation for the Latin word *post meridiem*, meaning past midday

radioactive elements elements that release particles of energy

relative dating estimation of fossil age by comparing to other fossils in layers of rock

sundial instrument used to tell time using the shadows cast by the sun

theory of special relativity physical theory of space and time developed by Albert Einstein that led to theories of time travel

time zone any of the 24 divisions of Earth's surface in which a standard time is kept

universal time time based on the Greenwich Mean Time

variable measurement that can change

Find out more

Books

No-sweat Science: Simple Experiments in Time, Muriel Mandell (Sterling, 2007)

True Stories: The Story Behind Time, Elizabeth Raum (Heinemann Library, 2009)

Websites

BBC skillswise
http://www.bbc.co.uk/skillswise/numbers/measuring/time/timesanddates/
Learn more about time and dates at this website.

BBC schools
http://www.bbc.co.uk/schools/ks2bitesize/maths/shape_space/measures/ read1.shtml
Learn all about measurements on this website.

Stop the clock!
http://resources.oswego.org/games/stoptheclock/sthec4.html
This is a simple game that allows you to practise converting digital times to analogue ones.

Place to visit

Science Museum
Exhibition Rd
South Kensington
London SW7 2DD
http://www.sciencemuseum.org.uk/visitmuseum/galleries/time_measurement. aspx
Visit the museum to see many different clocks.

Index